MONSTROUS MYTHS

Terrible Tales of
AFRICA

Clare Hibbert

Gareth Stevens
Publishing

Please visit our website, www.garethstevens.com. For a free color catalog of all our high-quality books, call toll free 1-800-542-2595 or fax 1-877-542-2596.

Library of Congress Cataloging-in-Publication Data

Hibbert, Clare.
Terrible tales of Africa / by Clare Hibbert.
 p. cm. — (Monstrous myths)
Includes index.
ISBN 978-1-4824-0196-7 (pbk.)
ISBN 978-1-4824-0197-4 (6-pack)
ISBN 978-1-4824-0194-3 (library binding)
1. Mythology, African — Juvenile literature. I. Hibbert, Clare, 1970-. II. Title.
BL2400.H53 2014
398.2—dc23

First Edition

Published in 2014 by
Gareth Stevens Publishing
111 East 14th Street, Suite 349
New York, NY 10003

Copyright © 2014 Arcturus Publishing

Illustrations: Janos Jantner (Beehive Illustration)
Editor: Joe Harris
Designer: Emma Randall
Cover designer: Emma Randall

Printed in the United States of America

CPSIA compliance information: Batch #CW14GS: For further information contact Gareth Stevens, New York, New York at 1-800-542-2595.

CONTENTS

African Stories..4

Anansi the Spiderman...6

Horrible Little Hlakanyana 10

The Big Bad Bird...14

The Cave of Bones 18

The Crafty Jackal..22

The Seven-Headed Serpent 26

Glossary 30

Further Information...31

Index 32

AFRICAN STORIES

Welcome to Africa, the world's second-largest continent, a land of sprawling deserts, dry grasslands, sweltering forests...and bustling cities!

At least 100 million Africans—that's one in ten—follow traditional African religions. Most of those people believe in one main, supreme god, who's too important to have much to do with people's day-to-day lives. Lesser deities and spirits get more involved with people's everyday goings-on, and they star in well-known African stories, too.

Crafty Hare is a trickster who crops up in stories in East and Central Africa.

Spirits are sometimes the ghosts of dead ancestors, who've spookily stuck around to protect their living relatives. They can also be other invisible beings, out to help or harm. Sometimes people try to control spirits using magic spells or special rituals. They might ask a priest, healer, or diviner to help them.

Although Africa has many different peoples and religions, some ideas crop up everywhere. There are loads of tales about talking animals, from lions and leopards to boa constrictors and baboons.

Tricksters such as Anansi the Spiderman, Jackal, and Hare are the cleverest animals of all. They use their cunning to outwit larger, more powerful creatures. Sometimes these animals are heroes or helpers, but occasionally their actions are rather silly!

Believe it or not!

The Ashanti people live in West Africa. Their storytellers always begin with the words: "We do not really mean, we do not really mean, that what we are going to say is true." It's their way of pointing out that the tale is make-believe.

ANANSI THE SPIDERMAN

Where did all the stories and myths come from? In West African mythology, they were a gift from Anansi the Spiderman. He reckoned they'd make those long evenings by the fire a bit more interesting. First, though, he had to buy them from Nyame, the sky god.

When Anansi asked Nyame to name his price for his box of stories, the god laughed like thunder until he realized Anansi was deadly serious.

Anansi was always getting himself into trouble!

"Okay, Spidey," he said. "Bring me four creatures and you can have the box." Easy? Not really. The creatures Nyame wanted were Onini the python, Osebo the leopard, Mmboro the hornet, and Mmoatia the invisible fairy. Anansi would need all his trickery to catch them!

First was Onini. Anansi approached the python's tree muttering, "She's wrong. He's way longer than this stick." As expected, Onini appeared.

"Just the fellow!" exclaimed Anansi, pretending to be surprised. "My wife insists you're shorter than this stick and won't believe how magnificently long you are."

"S-s-s-stupid s-s-s-spider!" grumbled Onini. "I'll ju-s-s-s-st lie next to the s-s-s-stick!"

When the python couldn't straighten out his coils, Anansi helpfully offered to hold him straight with his silken thread. And presto! The python was tied to the stick. "Now who's stupid, Onini?" laughed Anansi.

To catch Osebo the leopard, Anansi dug a deep pit. When the big cat fell in, Anansi offered to help him out. He lowered down a booby-trapped tree branch. When the leopard grabbed on, it spun him round by the tail and wrapped him up in silk! Two creatures down, two to go...

A leopard lollipop! I bet that surprised the sky god!

Anansi's next problem was Mmboro the hornet. Could he avoid getting a painful sting? Armed with a calabash of water and a big leaf, Anansi headed to the Mmboro's nest. He tipped half the water over his head, the rest over the nest, and then held up the leaf like an umbrella.

"Oh!" groaned Anansi as Mmboro and all the other hornets swarmed out. "The rains have come early. Shelter in my calabash if you want." But as the hornets buzzed in, Anansi trapped them using the leaf and some silk. Gift-wrapped hornets for Nyame!

Part-spider, part-man, Anansi is the main character in the many "spider stories" told in West Africa.

Anansi's last challenge was to capture Mmoatia, the invisible fairy. He coated a little doll with sticky gum and fixed thread to its head so he could make it nod like a puppet. Then he left it in a clearing with a dish of yummy yam paste—the fairy's favorite!

When Mmoatia found the doll, she asked if she could have some paste. She was delighted when it nodded! But she didn't have a reputation for bad temper for nothing. When the doll didn't answer her "Thank you!" she lashed out and stuck fast to the gum! After that, Anansi hauled the shrieking fairy up to Nyame.

BREAKING NEWS!
People Gather to Hear New Stories

There were celebrations today as people looked forward to their first-ever evening of storytelling – all thanks to Anansi. The clever spider did a deal with the sky god and now Nyame has handed over the box of stories. Hope you're all sitting comfortably!

Believe it or not!

The character of Anansi crossed to the Caribbean and Central America in the stories of slaves, who were shipped there from Africa. Now his spider stories are famous all over the world!

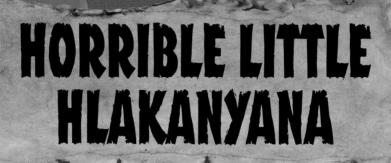

HORRIBLE LITTLE HLAKANYANA

Forget about little bundles of joy. This is the story of a chief and his wife who desperately wanted a child—and ended up with a miniature monster. One day, the chief decided to sacrifice an ox to see if that might bring them a baby. It sure did, but what a weird one! The "child" who turned up was Hlakanyana, a dangerous little trickster who'd existed since the dawn of time.

The chief had only just finished sacrificing the ox when Hlakanyana ran up and offered to help him. He said he would give out the meat to all the huts in the village. But then he took it all to his new mom's and left blood on the other people's mats. When they complained, Hlakanyana said the dogs must've stolen their meat.

Freaky Hlakanyana was born able to walk and talk, but had the face of an old, old man.

Soon after, Hlakanyana killed and ate two cows, then smeared the blood on one of the other village boys as he slept so that people thought he was the thief. What a tiny trouble-maker!

Hlakanyana's last exploit in that village was to raid the shared cooking pot, where an enormous ox head was stewing. He staged a robbery of all the other cattle to draw away the villagers while he gorged on the ox head. Then he framed a sleeping old man for the crime by leaving fat on his lips and a bone by his side.

Hlakanyana doesn't know about respecting the elderly. All he respects is his own belly!

This time, the villagers saw through Hlakanyana's trick and chased after him. But they didn't know about his supernatural powers. He simply changed himself into an old woman and pointed his pursuers in the wrong direction.

After that, horrible Hlakanyana had many adventures. On one occasion he tricked an old woman into a cooking pot by saying it would make her young again. When her sons found out, they chased him, but he escaped by turning into a stone.

In another village, Hlakanyana met a goatherd girl. It was love at first sight—love for tasty goat meat, that is! The greedy-guts married the girl and herded her goats...right into his bottomless pit of a stomach.

Another time, Hlakanyana offered to help Hyena finish building his house in return for sharing some meat. Then the wicked fiend wove Hyena's tail into the thatch of the roof and stole all the meat for himself!

Hungry Hlakanyana would eat absolutely anything...including live leopard cubs!

Next, Hlakanyana offered his babysitting services to a leopardess so she could go hunting. She was so hungry that she leaped on his offer. She didn't realize he had a taste for leopard-cub lunches! Once he'd eaten all her young, he ran again, with the frenzied leopardess hot on his heels.

Eventually Hlakanyana returned to his parents' village. He never stopped playing tricks, but the last laugh was on him. One day he offered a tired tortoise a ride on his back. Perhaps he meant to eat the tortoise, but for some reason it stuck fast, and he couldn't get the beast off. His poor old mom tried to help him by pouring on hot fat and succeeded, but also fried Hlakanyana alive. It was a slippery end for a very slippery customer!

Believe it or not!

The trickster Hlakanyana appears in the folklore of many African peoples, including the Zulu and Xhosa of southern Africa. Apart from his non-stop eating, Hlakanyana's other favorite activity is making up boastful songs about his cunning tricks.

THE BIG BAD BIRD

Imagine a huge bird with such a raging appetite that it could almost ruin a village. That's the monstrous creature that features in a favorite tale told by the people of Tanzania in East Africa.

The bird was truly beautiful, but its insatiable hunger was threatening the villagers with starvation.

The bird mysteriously arrived at the village, and it wasn't long before the people were racking their brains to find a way to get rid of it. Each night, it snatched goats and chickens and gobbled up every last plant out in the fields. Each day, while the villagers worked hard to replant the fields, the ravenous bird ransacked their winter food supplies. In the rare moments that it wasn't guzzling their food, the beastly bird sat high in an old yellowwood tree.

Eventually, the village chief decided that enough was enough. He told his people that they would have to chop down the tree to get rid of the bird. Fired up, the men of the village sharpened their axes and machetes and headed to the tree.

Will they force the feathered fiend to fly the coop? Well, let's just say you shouldn't count your chickens before they've hatched...

As the men landed the first blows on the tree trunk, the bird appeared and began to sing the sweetest, most enchanting song ever. It bewitched the men, reminding them of half-forgotten feelings and long-gone memories. The men crumbled, dropping their tools and falling to their knees in a trance. The longer they listened, the less the men could believe bad things of the bird. Eventually they shuffled back to the chief, dazed and confused. "We're sorry," they mumbled. "But we can't harm the bird!"

THE BIRD SPOTTERS' GUIDE TO THE BIGGEST BEAKED BEASTIES

Many birds' songs have been described as magical.... but in the case of this giant creature, it was literally true! Its trilling song could show people their fondest wishes. After the failure of the older men from the village, the younger men tried to chop down the tree. But when the bird began to sing, they dreamed of a wonderful future, in which they were famous heroes. When they came to their senses, they felt pretty silly.

The chief decided that the children of the village were their last chance. "Children can hear truly and see clearly," he said. But was this just wishful thinking? As the children began to chop, the menacing bird appeared once more, and it sang one last song.

For once, no one told the kids off for not listening properly—it was absolutely the right thing to do. Even the chief grew weak as the song went on, but the children took no notice! They just chopped and chopped until, eventually, the trunk began to crack. The mighty old yellowwood crashed to the ground, crushing the bird under its weight. The village was free from the big bad bird, and it was all thanks to the children!

Chop! Chop! Chop! The children were so busy with what they were doing that they didn't fall under the bird's spell.

Believe it or not!

The menacing bird is a popular tale with Bantu-speaking peoples. They hold traditional folk beliefs. When villagers have a problem, they visit a healer, who helps them ward off evil magic and spirits.

THE CAVE OF BONES

Everyone knows that Lion is the king of the beasts. He's a big-shot predator that no animal would ever dare to cross. But in South Africa, traditional tales tell of how, once upon a time, Lion was even scarier than he is today...because he could fly!

Flying Lion was a beast with mighty wings and claws as hard as iron.

Flying Lion's wings weren't feathered or furred—they were covered in thick strong skin, like a bat's. When he went out hunting, Flying Lion would soar through the air, surveying the land below for a decent meal. When he spotted a herd, he didn't need to pick off the weakest and oldest animals from the fringes. He picked out the biggest, juiciest specimen and just swooped on down and caught it.

There was only one thing that Flying Lion was afraid of: the bones in his cave being broken. No one knew why. All they knew was that Flying Lion's cave floor was piled high with the bones of every animal he'd ever killed and eaten, and that he employed a pair of white crows to guard them.

The white crows weren't terribly bright. The term 'bird-brained' was probably invented for them...

One day, while Flying Lion was off hunting, Big Bullfrog turned up at the cave. He said that he'd watch the bones for a while, if the crows wanted to go and stretch their wings. The crazy crows didn't realize that it was all a trick! Big Bullfrog wanted to know why Flying Lion didn't want the bones broken. And to find out, he was going to break them and see what happened!

When the white crows saw that Big Bullfrog had broken all the bones, they were petrified. They flew after him to find out why on earth he'd put them in such terrible danger. But Big Bullfrog just hopped on home. "Tell Flying Lion that I broke the bones," he declared. "And that he can find me by the pond."

Big Bullfrog knew that the only place that he could safely face Lion was beside water. With just one leap, he could make a speedy getaway.

Meanwhile, far away, Flying Lion had singled out a zebra to snatch. His sly smile turned to gaping horror when he discovered that his wings had stopped working. He plodded all the way home, where he found the white crows, half-dead with fright. Their fear soon disappeared when they realized that Flying Lion was just plain Lion now. When he threatened to bite off their heads, they easily dodged his leaps. Just before they flew off for good, they told him about Big Bullfrog.

Lion headed over to the pond and crept up on his enemy. But as he pounced, Big Bullfrog dove into the water and came up the other side. This happened over and over until finally Lion realized he'd never catch Bullfrog in a million years.

Poor old Lion went home and tried to mend the broken bones, but it was no good. And without the bones kept whole, he couldn't fly and he couldn't dive-bomb his prey. Lion had to learn to creep quietly and stealthily, and that's how he's hunted ever since.

Believe it or not!

Flying Lion is often known as Oom Leeuw, which is Afrikaans for "Uncle Lion." Afrikaans is a language of Dutch origin, spoken across southern Africa. Many African myths feature the lion, usually as the ruler of the animals.

THE CRAFTY JACKAL

Real jackals have a crafty way of getting fed—they wait for lions to make a kill and then mob them, stealing the meal. The jackal of southern African folk tales is just as cunning and just as lazy, and he, too, outwits a lion.

The story begins with a terrible drought. The king of the beasts called together all the animals and they agreed to dig a hole to collect the next rains. The only animal that didn't join in the digging was Jackal. He didn't want to get all hot, dirty, and thirsty.

Sneaky Jackal was always dreaming up new ways to trick the other animals.

Soon after, the rains came and filled the waterhole. And who was the first to come and drink? Jackal, of course! He even took a dip, leaving the water all muddy and disgusting.

When Jackal came back to do the same the next day, he found Baboon guarding the waterhole. But crafty Jackal knew Baboon had a sweet tooth, so he pretended that his clay pot was full of honey. "De-licious!" he exclaimed, licking his paw. "I don't want any of their dirty water when I've got all this yummy honey!"

Bumbling Baboon fell right into Jackal's trap. He begged and begged for honey, and eventually Jackal said he could have some... so long as he handed over his fighting stick and let Jackal tie him up. Baboon stupidly agreed.

Don't do it, Baboon, you great hairy ape! Surely even you can see that this is a trick?

Once Baboon was all tied up, Jackal drank the water, filled his pot, and swam about as Baboon looked miserably on. "I don't have any honey!" gloated Jackal. "All you'll get from me is a swipe with your own stick!"

When the animals found Baboon trussed up like a turkey, Lion was not pleased. Then Tortoise offered to catch Jackal. Everyone thought he was joking—he could barely outrun a snail! But Tortoise had a plan. He covered himself in sticky resin till he resembled a big black stone. Then he waited by the waterhole. Sure enough, Jackal stepped on the "stone" and became stuck! "Let's see you wriggle out of this one," muttered Tortoise. It was time for a trial...

Courtroom Notes: Trial of Jackal

The court gathered to hear the case of Jackal, accused of stealing water, muddying water and making Baboon look silly. All rose for Judge Lion. Jackal was found guilty on all three counts and sentenced to a death of his choosing. Unusually, the defendant chose being swung around by his shaved and greased tail, then having his brains dashed out on a stone. Sentence will be carried out by Hyena tomorrow.

Of course, the minute Hyena tried to grab his tail, Jackal slipped from his grasp and ran off, with Lion in hot pursuit. An overhanging rock gave Jackal the idea for one last cunning plan. He made himself look as if he was stopping the rock from rolling down and crushing him and Lion. Without thinking, Lion joined Jackal to help hold up the rock. After a while, Jackal offered to go and fetch something to prop it up. No prizes for guessing whether he came back!

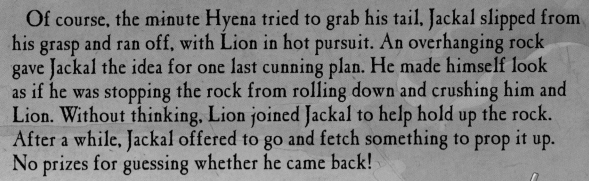

Believe it or not!

In another version of this story, the trickster is a hare, and the animals are guarding a store of fat, rather than a pool of water.

Hyena didn't stand a chance of keeping his grip on Jackal!

THE SEVEN-HEADED SERPENT

Once there was a woman called Manjuza. She was so talented at singing and dancing that she became a wedding dancer. Whenever someone got married, they asked Manjuza to break out her dance moves and get the party started.

Not everyone was a fan of Manjuza. She was about to become the victim of some bad magic...

One day, an old woman asked Manjuza to dance at her granddaughter's wedding, but Manjuza had already promised to be at someone else's. She said that if the old woman could change the day then she'd happily dance at both weddings. But the woman wasn't used to not having her own way. She spitefully cast a curse on Manjuza's husband, Mthiyane. When he returned from his hunting trip, she cackled, he'd be a monster.

What a wicked old witch! Doesn't she know that it's bad manners to curse?

Poor Manjuza sat up waiting for Mthiyane to return. Eventually, just before dawn, he came home. But he looked odd. His eyes were flashing, and his tongue was lolling out of his mouth. As Manjuza watched in horror, her beloved husband turned into a snake with seven heads.

Manjuza realized that their three children would soon wake up. Thinking fast, she hid the snake in a big black pot inside one of the winter storehouses. When the children asked for their father, Manjuza said he'd be away a few more days.

That night, after she'd cried herself to sleep, Manjuza had a dream. Her grandmother appeared to her, telling her that all she had to do to break the curse was dance at seven weddings. When she came back from the seventh wedding, Mthiyane would be back in his own body. But she must keep all this a secret, even from her own children.

Manjuza threw herself into the dance challenge! And soon she neared her target of seven weddings. However, in the meantime, the children noticed that there was something mysterious about one of the huts. Why did their mother keep it locked? And why did she look so troubled?

A talking, seven-headed snake? Everyone in the village would be terrified if it got loose...

The day of the seventh wedding dawned and Manjuza left the children at home to play. They tried the hut door—as they had so many times before—but this time it opened! Manjuza had forgotten to lock it! Lifting the lid of the pot, the children came face to face with the seven-headed snake. Aaaagh! They screamed and ran away, while the snake slithered down to the riverbank.

Soon a band of kids gathered around the snake. They discovered that not only did it have seven heads, but that each head spoke. Terrified, they told their moms and dads. The dads suggested leaving the snake alone. After all, it might be a sign from their ancestors.

The moms took matters into their own hands. They charged down to the river and threw hot porridge all over the monster until its skin blistered and its body shuddered and went still.

As Manjuza returned home, she heard the women singing by the river about killing a snake. She approached, full of dread, but as she watched, her dear husband rose up from the blistered body, looking sleepy and confused. The curse had been lifted after all!

Believe it or not!

The Xhosa people who tell the tale of Manjuza believe seven is a magical number. Seven crops up in the myths of other cultures, too. Seven-headed dragons appear in the legends of southern Asia, the Middle East, the Mediterranean, and Celtic Britain.

GLOSSARY

ancestor Someone who lived long ago, from whom others are descended.

Bantu The name for a group of closely related languages spoken by peoples in eastern and southern Africa. There may be as many as 600 different ethnic groups in Africa that speak Bantu languages.

booby-trap To set up an object so that it turns into a surprising trap.

calabash The fruit of the bottle gourd tree, which can be hollowed out and used as a container for carrying liquids.

chief The most important person in a tribe (community of people).

deity A god or goddess.

demon An evil spirit.

diviner Someone who has special contact with spirits and gods and who uses their power to predict future events.

drought A time when there is little or no rainfall.

healer Someone who has special contact with spirits and gods and who uses their power to help people who are sick.

insatiable Impossible to satisfy.

machete A wide, weighty knife.

metropolis A large city.

predator An animal that kills other animals for food.

pursuer Someone chasing someone else.

ravenous Extremely hungry.

resin A sticky substance produced by the trunk of a tree or bush.

ritual A ceremony that involves a particular set of actions.

sacrifice To give something as an offering to the gods or spirits.

slave A person who belongs to another person and is forced to work for them for no money.

supernatural Belonging to the world of spirits and gods, rather than the natural world.

trickster A character who cheats or deceives others. Anansi and Jackal are two tricksters in African stories.

trussed Tied.

wedding dancer Someone who performs ritual dances at weddings for a living.

yam A starchy vegetable.

yellowwood A large evergreen tree.

FURTHER INFORMATION

Further Reading

Africa Is Not a Country by Margy Burns Knight and Mark Melnicove (Millbrook Press, 2002)

African Art and Culture by Jane Bingham (Raintree, 2008)

African Myths by Neil Morris (Franklin Watts, 2012)

Favorite African Folktales edited by Nelson Mandela (W.W. Norton, 2007)

Folk Tales from Africa: The Baboons Who Went This Way and That by Alexander McCall Smith (Canongate Books, 2006)

Websites

anansistories.com
A collection of traditional stories about the trickster hero, Anansi.

www.bbc.co.uk/worldservice/africa/features/storyofafrica/
An overview of cultures in Africa from the BBC World Service, plus a link to a radio program on the subject.

www.godchecker.com/pantheon/african-mythology.php?_gods-list
An A–Z database with descriptions of nearly 200 African gods.

www.worldoftales.com/
Links to 88 different African folk tales and more.

Publisher's note to educators and parents: Our editors have carefully reviewed these websites to ensure that they are suitable for students. Many websites change frequently, however, and we cannot guarantee that a site's future contents will continue to meet our high standards of quality and educational value. Be advised that students should be closely supervised whenever they access the Internet.

INDEX

Afrikaans 21
Anansi the Spiderman 5, 6–9

baboons 5, 23, 24
Bantu 17
Big Bad Bird 14–17
Big Bullfrog 19–21

Central Africa 4

East Africa 4, 14

Flying Lion 18–21

gods 4, 6

Hare 4, 5, 25
healers 5, 17
Hlakanyana 10–13
Hyena 12, 24, 25

Jackal 5, 22–25

leopards 5, 7, 13
lions 5, 18–21, 22, 23–25

Manjuza 26–29
Mmboro the hornet 7, 8
Mmoatia 7, 9
Mthiyane 27

Nyame 6–9

Onini the python 7
Osebo the leopard 7

religions 4, 5

slaves 11
snakes
    boa constrictor 5
    python 7
    seven-headed 27–29
South Africa 18
Southern Africa 13, 21, 22
spirits 4, 5, 17

Tanzania 14
tortoises 13, 24

West Africa 5, 6, 8

Xhosa 13, 29

zebras 21
Zulu 13